Enemy at the Gate

Enemy at the Gate

❖

Raphael Grant

Copyright © 2018 by Raphael Grant.

Library of Congress Control Number:		2018910428
ISBN:	Hardcover	978-1-9845-5131-3
	Softcover	978-1-9845-5130-6
	eBook	978-1-9845-5129-0

All rights reserved. No part of this book may be reproduced or transmitted in any form or by any means, electronic or mechanical, including photocopying, recording, or by any information storage and retrieval system, without permission in writing from the copyright owner.

Scripture quotations marked KJV are from the Holy Bible, King James Version (Authorized Version). First published in 1611. Quoted from the KJV Classic Reference Bible, Copyright © 1983 by The Zondervan Corporation.

Scripture quotations marked NIV are taken from the Holy Bible, New International Version®. NIV®. Copyright © 1973, 1978, 1984 by International Bible Society. Used by permission of Zondervan. All rights reserved. [Biblica]

Scripture quotations marked NKJV are taken from the New King James Version. Copyright © 1982 by Thomas Nelson, Inc. Used by permission. All rights reserved.

Any people depicted in stock imagery provided by Getty Images are models, and such images are being used for illustrative purposes only.
Certain stock imagery © Getty Images.

Print information available on the last page.

Rev. date: 09/4/2018

To order additional copies of this book, contact:
Xlibris
1-888-795-4274
www.Xlibris.com
Orders@Xlibris.com
781485

CONTENTS

Acknowledgement vii
Dedication ix
Introduction xi

What Is A Gate 1
Reasons For The Gates 3
Understanding Gates 5
Rules Of Engagement, Spiritual Warfare 12
There Are Different Kinds Of Gates 14
Possesing Time 19
Understanding The Gate Of Time 23
Prayer Watches 25
The Eight Prayer Watches 27
Spiritual Warfare 36
The Opposers 38
The Battle 41
The Battle Is The Lord 43
The Weapon Of Our Warfare 45
Ready Or Not….. You're In The Battle 46
The God Of This Age 48

Strategies Of The Devil 50
Condemnation Of The Devil 53
Painting Doubt 55
Fear 57
Satan Thoughts And Imaginations 59
Depression 61
Be Careful Of Who Stands At Your Gate 63
Satanic Gates 65
Entering Into New Gates 68
Understand The Spiritual Realm 70

ACKNOWLEDGEMENT

I want to express my deep thanks and profound gratitude to Jacky Fobi Tamo for the sacrifice of Labor she put into the type setting of this, the blessing will be unending.

DEDICATION

I dedicate this book to my best friend, lover and Wife Aretha Grant. You have always been there, even when it is difficult, and hard. You are absolutely amazing.

To my boys Zuriel and Zephan, you always make me proud, you are the kind of children that any parent will ask God for, I love you so much and there is absolutely nothing I can do about it.

INTRODUCTION

Couple of years ago, the Lord spoke to me about gates, it happened that one faithful day I went to the church office, when I entered into the church headed towards my office, while climbing the stairs the Lord spoke to me audibly "enemy at the gate" twice. I didn't understand, I contemplated and pondered over it all day what that means and what the Lord was trying to tell me. As I pondered over the word, the Lord spoke to me again and said there is an enemy at the gate of the church, and until the enemy is removed, the church will not grow numerically, and at the time, the congregation of the church was fast declining, and so I thought there was somebody spiritually standing at the gate of the church expelling the church members and preventing new ones from coming in.

To my amazement the Lord told me that it was my personal assistant, the church secretary, I asked how and why? The Lord said she is the doorway to the church and also the exit, anybody coming to the church and needs information concerning the church, when they call the church office it's the secretary that answers it, and determine if the person should come or not, based on the information she gives or what she says to the person. Apparently when people call the church, the secretary will tell them not to come to church.

I started studying on gates, physical gates and spiritual gates, I fired the secretary immediately, and the growth of the church started.

Please stay with me as I embark on this spiritual journey, it will enlighten you and illuminate your understanding.

What Is A Gate

Gates and doors are very significant in the life of human beings. A city without a gate is open to various unwanted things and personalities. Just as in the physical, there are also spiritual gates and doors.

Gates are designed to leave a firm control of entry and exit into a house, city, apartments, or institution. We live in a day where our nation's border control has become the major topic of politicians and many other civilians. The reason is because, we want to control what comes in and what goes out, the borders of the nation. It is the gate of our nation, and if it is not firmly controlled evil and calamity, can come in and affect our nation and the people there in. This means gates are erected so that one can limit and restrict what comes in and out, not only that but to also know what comes in and out.

As an Intercessor, you are the gateman of your family, job, house, and your city. You have the power on your knees to grant access or deny. On your knees you have the ability to lock in friends and to lock out enemies from coming in. As believers our spiritual gates are the prayers we pray, to open doors for blessings, favor, healing, breakthrough and the rest. When we cease to stand at the gate of prayer, we allow evil spirits and forces of darkness to come into our home, life, and our destiny to tear us apart.

A gate is any port of access used for the purpose of both entry and exit. This is not only in the natural but also in the spiritual realm, the realm of soul or the realm of the physical. Gates can be visible and invisible and we must become aware of when we face a gate.

- <u>Physical gate are made of different building materials, some are metal while others are wood.</u>

Reasons For The Gates

I. Gates are not just erected or designed, gates are built technically to increase security due to potential danger of the invaluable and precious things that are within the gates, which is why most often equipment and gadgets such as censor lights, luggage scanners, and cameras are used to restrict any unwanted device from gaining entry.

II. It is for the purpose of human reinforcement; vigilantes, armed with weapon or rungus, security men, military men, gate keepers, and watchmen.

III. Legal reinforcement: In some cases and incidences there are firm visible written warning made against trespasser beyond the gate will be legal action.

There are certain violent and consequent attack over cities and nation in some parts of our world, that has propel, an extreme measures where barricades are erected around families and homes, and even schools reinforce security

Understanding Gates

Gates are designed to protect the people in the city and to keep the enemy out from invading and intrusion, in biblical times, gates were places of merchandise, it was a place of high transactions of business and it was also the centrality of every high profile activity, such as announcements, judgements, and conveyance of court proceedings.

That is why the bible rampantly talks and speak of "sitting and standing at the gates" referring to activities taking place at the gate.

If you don't prevail against the spiritual gates, you won't prevail against the spiritual gates, until the spiritual is opened the physical gate will never open, the authority of the spiritual gate supersedes that of the physical gate.

You must understand that every gate has guards controlling who comes in and who goes out, meaning they have power over who exits and who enters the gate, and if you have an evil and wicked man at the gate, then you are in trouble; he will close the gate when you are supposed to be entering and will make you exit when you are supposed to be staying in the gate.

To possess the gate of the enemy, you must be militant and aggressive in warfare, satanic guard don't easily relinquish the gate, it takes violence and force to let go, and that can only be done through consistence and persistence in prayer.

> *"She cries out in the chief concourses, at the opening of the gates in the city"*
> (Proverbs 1:21)

Wisdom is personified, for her wisdom to be heard by multitudes she needs to speak at the gate, were people from all walks of life has gathered. At the gate she also make petition and requests, because she know that it is a place of influence and power, desires are granted at the gate and wish come to pass at the gate.

The foundation of any kingdom is composed. This is why battles fought are usually won or lost at the gates. To destroy anything successfully you need to go to its foundation. To take and conquer any place or kingdom, you will need to take the gates.

The first mention of the city gate is found in the book of beginning.

> *"Now the two angels came to Sodom in the evening, and Lot was sitting in the gate of Sodom. When Lot saw them, he rose to meet them, and he bowed himself with his face towards the ground."*
> (Genesis 19:1)

Lot greeted the angels not in his house, but at the gate of Sodom, which he was there with other sodomites and foreigners engaging in business transactions and civil issues.

> *"And they blessed Rebekah and said unto her, thou art our sister, be thou the mother of thousands of millions, and let thy seed possess the gate of those which hate them."*
> (Genesis 24:60)

When we possess the gates of our enemies or the gates of hell, we possess the entire territory, not just a particular structure.

> *"And it happened as the gate was being shut, when it was dark that the men went out. Where the men went I do not know; pursue them quickly, for you may overtake them."*
>
> (Joshua 2:5)

Because they were the chief point from which the enemy attacked (Judges 5:8). Idolatrous acts were performed at the gates (Acts 14:13). Battering rams were set against the gates (Ezekiel 21:22) and the gates were broken down and burned with fire (Nehemiah 1:3). The gates were seats of authority (Ruth 4:11). At the gates wisdom was uttered (Proverbs 1:21). Judges and officers served at the gates administering Justice (Deuteronomy 16:18) and the councils of state were held at the gates (2 chronicles 18:9). The word was read (Nehemiah 8:2-3) and the prophets proclaimed God's message (Jeremiah 17:19-20) from the gates. The people also had to enter through the gates to worship the Lord.

In the scriptures, gates were not only found in cities, but also in camps, houses, temples and palaces. We as God's people are called the dwelling place of God. The human body is called the tent or temple for the Holy Spirit. There are many scriptures that speak about the gates. Gates in the natural are something that you enter trough. The same is true in the spiritual. Every person has gates to their spirit, soul and body. The Word tells us that when we receive Jesus we are sealed with the Holy Spirit in our spirit. The gates to our spirit are closed when our spirit become a new creation.

> "There for Jesus said again, I tell you the truth, I am the gate for the sheep."
> (John 10:7 (NIV))

> "I am the way the truth and the life. No one comes to the father except through me."
> (John 14:6 (NIV))

Satan's kingdom's mirrors everything in God's kingdom, producing a counterfeit. There if there is gate to heaven there is most assuredly a gate to hell.

> "And I tell you that you are Peter, and on this rock I will build my church, and the gates of Hades will not overcome it."
> (Matthew 16:18 (NIV))

Jesus said the way to the Father and salvation is narrow. However the opposite is true about entering the enemy's path. There are many gates on Satan's road, and they all lead a person to destruction.

> "Enter through the narrow gate. For wide is the gate and broad is the road that leads to destruction, and many enter through it. But small is the gate and narrow the road that leads to life and only a few find it."
> (Matthew 7:13-14 (NIV))

We all must actively choose to identify and tear down mental strongholds and likewise not allow the enemy to access us through our doors and gates. Our perceptions of our life situations, the patterns and beliefs that we operate in and how we feed either our flesh or our spirit man are all of great importance.

This is not only to tear down strongholds but to guards the doors and gates that allow deception to enter and turn us to the wrong direction. We want to have the mind of Christ, so guard your doors and gates and tear down strongholds that are contrary to the word of God. Let God be your stronghold.

In the Law of Moses disobedient son's parent were asked to bring him to the city gate, for the elders to check and look at the evidence before passing judgement (Deuteronomy 21:18-21). This action confirms that the city gate is the paramount place for community activity. In the book of Ruth 4: 1-11, Boaz became officially a kinsman-redeemer by the meeting of the elders at the Bethlehem gate that is where the legabities of his marriage to Ruth was done.

"When he mentioned the Ark of God, Eli fell back from his seat by the gate, broke his neck and died; For he was an aged man and heavy for 40 years he had judged Israel" (I Samuel 4:8)

So this scripture points to the fact that Eli died at the gate. In the Ancient times military instructions and strategies are done at the gates. David gave his mighty men instructions as the ruler and King of Israel at the gate. (2 Samuel 18 1-5).

Rules Of Engagement, Spiritual Warfare

When comes to spiritual warfare, you must was with revelation and battle with skill, if you are going to prevail, especially against the gates.

i. The first rule in spiritual warfare is to locate the enemy, without locating the enemy you lose your target.
ii. You must locate the source of the enemy strength.
iii. You must also know the power base of the enemy, which is the 3rd rule. This includes alters, gates, covenants, devices and keys that the enemy has been using. For Pharaoh, his power base was the Nile River.
iv. The fourth rule is to assess his strength relative to your strength. Our strength, as we have leant in the first lesson comes from God. He is Omnipotent. Once we have gained victory

over your enemy, we must then occupy that space or territory.

It is now necessary for us to deal with the gates. We have to deal with the gates of hell. Our lack of watchfulness has given ground to the enemy (the devil). He has become king in our homes, in our government, in our schools, in science and technology, in the media, in business, in the arts, sports and culture,

There Are Different Kinds Of Gates

- Gates can be in the physical realm:

    - Windows
    - Doors
    - Literal gates
    - Our hearts, eyes, mouths, ears, feet and hands
    - Television sets, telephones, radios and computers.

- Since all gates are not physical, you might not always need to enter literal gates.

- Gates are places where alters, thrones and dominions are set.

"Now it came to pass on the third day that Esther put on her royal apparel, and stood in

the inner court of the King's house, over against the king's house: and the king sat upon his royal house, over against the gate of the house"
(Esther 5:1)

For more reference, please see:

Jeremiah 38:7

- Gates are also decision making places.
- They are also immigration posts or security check points.

"In those days while Mordecai sat in the king's gate, two of the king's chamberlains, Bigthan and Teresh, of those which kept the door, were wroth, and sought to lay hands on the king Ahasuerus"
(Esther 2:21)

–Daniel 10:12-21

- Gates are places for transactions: business, legal, marital

"Then went **Boaz** up to the gate, and sat him down there: and, behold, the kinsman of whom Boaz spake came by; unto whom he said, Ho, such a one! Turn aside sit down here. And he turned aside, and sat down.

- There are also gates of heavens. Everything that we see in the physical realm first, happens and is controlled from the realm of the spirit.

- The societal gate – family, church, religion, government, economy/business, education, science and technology.

  - The Family gate gives you access to the earth. Religion gives you access to God. Government gives you access to the system that runs a nation. The business gate gives you access to trade and commerce. Etc.
  - Education opens the door for the transfer of knowledge, facts, thoughts, ideas skills and values.

- Roads are also access points. Any road is a gate because it is a port of access to some places for both entry and exit from that place.

Road junctions are more important gates than the single road since, here, two or more roads meet. Major round-abouts or crossroads will give or deny you access to some roads or some points on the roads.

- Then there are gates of the earth.

"Praise the Lord from the earth, you great sea creatures and all the depth; Fire and hail, snow and clouds; stormy wind, fulfilling his word, mountains and hills, fruitful trees and all cedars. Beast and all cattle; creeping things and flying fowl, kings of the earth and all peoples, Princes and all judges of the earth, both young men and maidens, old men and children. Let them praise the name of the Lord, for His name above is exalted, His glory is above the earth and heaven.
(Psalm 148:7-13)

- Great sea creatures
- All ocean depths
- Lightning and hail
- Snow and cloud
- Stormy and winds.

- The atmosphere is a gateway.
- Nations are gateways.
- Alters are gateways.
- Then there are the gates of life which include the body, soul and spirit.
- There is also the information gate.
- There is also death gate.
- Walls and boundaries – national and international boundaries.
- The tribal and language gates.

We need to learn how to possess gates because whoever possesses the gate controls the gate. When we possess the gate we change the environment or spiritual equation in the city, our lives and our families. We also change the atmosphere. The result of possessing the gates is that you can now dictate what happens in the place, therefore changing the laws, rulings, judgments and behavioral patterns. Possessing the gates of the enemy is part of kingdom lifestyle.

Possesing Time

We must understand therefore that the whole of creation Is measured by time. Everything goes through the gates of time. When it comes to individuals, everybody goes through the gates of time. That is, everybody had to pass through yesterday to get to today, and we will have to pass through today to get to tomorrow. The bible instructs us that there is time for everything and every matter there is a reason under the sun.

> *"And hath made of one blood all nations of men for to dwell on all the face of the earth, and hath determined the times before appointed, and the bounds of their habitation."*
>
> (Acts 17:26)

For more reference, please see:

(Ecclesiastes 8:5-6)
(Psalm 104:30)
(Genesis 1:1-5)

The first thing that God said was "Let there be light", and there was light. God called the light Day and the darkness Night. Therefore time has a limit to it; and time becomes a measure of all creation. Time is important to the Islamic religion. They have also spread their prayer times to remember Allah over the Watches.

It is essential to possess the gates of time. Divine timing is essential. Moments are the gateway to seconds, and seconds, are the gateway to days; days are gateways to weeks; weeks to months; months to seasons; seasons to years; years to decades; decades to generations; generations are gateway to centuries; Centuries to millennia; and millennia to eternity.

If we can possess the hour, that will possess the watch and we will then own the day. The first month of the season becomes the gate of the season, while the first season of the year becomes the gate of the year (and so on). That is why we lose generational blessing. There are access points to the gates of time. These are the imaginary lines drawn around the earth known as longitudes and latitudes.

> *"Their line is gone out through all the earth and their words to the end of the world. In them hath he sat a tabernacle for the sun."*
>
> (Psalm 19:4)

These lines are the summary of the gates of time on earth. The earth is a sphere; it is made up of 360 degrees. Now one degree is equivalent to four minutes. Multiplying the four minutes by 360 would give you 1440 minutes. 1440 minutes divided by 60 minutes gives you the 24 hour day – 12 hours in the day and 12 at night. One degree to the east or the west would give you 720 minutes. Dividing by 60 minutes gives you 12 hours.

The moon marks both spiritual and physical seasons. It could mark seasons of positive and negative influence, such as seasons of grace and disgrace; seasons of glory and shame; and seasons of promotion and demotion. That is why it is imperative for us to control the gate of the time. Job asks in Job 38:12. *"Hast thou command the morning since thy days; and caused the dayspring to know his place."*

The sad thing is that the whole of out calendar is pagan. Our days and months are named after roman gods:

1. Sunday was named after the sun.
2. Monday was named after the moon.
3. Tuesday was named after the war god, Mars.
4. Wednesday was named after the god Mercury.

5. Thursday was named after Thor, the god of thunder.
6. Friday was named after Frigga.
7. Saturday was named after Saturn.

- March was named after the god of war, Mars.
- January was named after Janus – The gate of the year has now become January.

The romans therefore still control the world. The empire that is to control the world started as the club of Rome. It has evolved into the European Union. I have said all these to under pin the fact that we need to take up a watch before the Lord. There watches were set out as a time set apart by God, a time for Christians to take hold of the day and night (because there is a 24 hour day split up into a 12 hour day and a 12 hour night.)

Please see:
(Judges 7:19)
(Isaiah 62:6-7)
(Jeremiah 51:13)

Understanding The Gate Of Time

When you catch the understanding and revelation of the gate of time, you will discover the gates of time and possess them, you will possess everything else. We need to possess the key to the knowledge of the gate of time. Time itself can be redeemed.

The very first second of the minute becomes the gateway to that minute, and that is what we must possess. Again the first minute becomes the gateway to the hour, hour to the watch and watch to the day, day to the week, week to the beginning of the new month. You have to possess the gates of time.

Please see: (Ecclesiastes 8:5-6)

On the first day, light was created, when it comes to individuals, everybody goes through the gates of time, to pass through yesterday to get to today and to pass through today to get to get to tomorrow. There is time for everything; and for every matter, there is a season under the sun.

Please see:
(Acts 17:26)
(Proverbs 16:33)

Those things that are seen today were made out of the things which do not appear.

They existed in other realm of experience, that is, the realm of the spirit and this realm is beyond time.

There is an appointed and appropriate time for everything. So what God does to any individual or nation is at the appointed time or at least in the fullness of time.

Please see: (Ecclesiastes 3: 1-8)

Prayer Watches

"Their line is gone out through all the earth and their words to the end of the world. In them hath he set a tabernacle for the sun."

(Psalm 19:4)

Earth is made up of 360 degrees – 1 degree = 4 minutes. 1440 minutes divided by 60 = 24 hours. Every citizen of the kingdom of God is supposed to understand the gates of time. We are to pray through the watches – guard and protect the watches.

There are eight watches, four watches for the day and four watches for the night.

Please see:
(Psalm 90: 4)
(Jeremiah 6: 4)

This is the time for covenants – a time of renewal of covenant. It's a time for the release of divine beginnings, so God has to deal with all the wrong foundations in your life.

- In your family
- In the church
- In government
- In the Economy
- In science and technology
- In formal schools
- In the media
- In the Arts, Sports and cultures.

Pray that God will lead the church to subdue all spiritual and physical strongholds that constitute the kingdom of darkness, strongholds of false religious bodies in our nations; Strongholds of divinations; and strongholds of witchcraft.

The Eight Prayer Watches

1. First Watch: (6:00 pm TO 9:00 pm)

This is the time for self-examination, were you come to God with a repentant heart asking for forgiveness and mercy, it is the time for self-evaluation and meditation. At this watch the Sun is setting the Jews believe according to their tradition, it is the end of the previous day and rising of a new day. At this watch, you allow the Holy Spirit to search your heart and mind, to blot out your transgression and sin, it is the time of absolute humility in his presence. This is the time we come to divine alignment with the counsel and divine purpose of God. This is the watch that Almighty God strengthen us and empower our inner most being for the task ahead. It is a time for absolute Focus and concertation on the Lord to uproot every distraction from our mind and heart.

You must also understand that this watch also focuses on the future, and also at this time you decree and declare your future and destiny, taking control of your destiny and purpose, placing a demand on heaven for the manifestation of your destiny. At this watch you make divine utterances for provision and blessings.

During this time you appropriate the covenant blessing of the Almighty God, asking for speedily fruition of his covenanted blessings. This is the hour of dedication and full consecration to the Almighty God.

2. Second Watch (9:00 PM to Midnight)

"But about midnight Paul and Silas were praying and singing hymns to God, and the prisoners were listening to them. Then suddenly a tremendous earthquake occurred, which shook the prison to its foundation. At once all the doors sprang open and every one's chains fell off" (Acts 16:25-26) **NKJV**.

"At midnight I will rise to give thanks to you, because of your righteous judgement. (Psalm 119:62).

During this time, we root out and completely destroy satanic foundations designed to confine, limit, and restrict us from achieving our divine purpose and mandate, through prayer and praise.

You see Paul and Silas were in prison and the prison that they were placed in was designed to stop them from accomplishing their assignment and mission for their life and they knew it. The scripture says they praised and prayed at midnight and the foundation shook and the shackles were broken. At this prayer watch you invoke righteous judgement over situations, conditions, and circumstances that are not in alignment with the Will of God for your life, ministry, family and our destiny. This watch is the hour were angels are released into the earth to enforce the will and the counsel of God for our lives, it is also a time for supernatural and angelic encounters. This is the watch that captives are set free, it is the hour of deliverance and total emancipation from the powers of darkness, through fervent prayer and praise warfare.

3. Third Watch (12 Midnight to 3AM)

This is the time when witches and wizards meet, to destroy, to kill, to steal, and to cast spells. It is also the time when witches plant demonic seeds into our ministry, families, career, and destiny to abort the purpose of God for our lives.

This is the time witches manipulate our marriages and spiritually hijacking our blessings and prosperity, this is not the hour of amatures and novice, this is the prayer watch of intense spiritual warfare and prayer destroying the works of satanic world and witchcraft, dismantling their power base and commanding fire to burn and consume them.

4. The Fourth Watch (3:00 AM to 6:00 AM)

During this watch, you exercise dominion and authority over creation. It is this watch, where we experience supernatural activities, divine intervention in our lives. It is during this watch, we exercise superior authority over the elements and decreeing the Lordship of Christ here on earth. This is the hour, which we are to function and operate by Faith and the Supernatural, in the face of opposition, resistance, and adversity, we stand courageous with inner boldness and tenacity.

At this watch, you declare the beauty and goodness of God into your life by releasing new favor, new elevations, new opportunities, new mercies and new grace.

This is the watch that you command, your blessings, you turn your mourning into dancing, and you speak and command your morning to come into being.

"Hast Thou commanded the morning since thy days, and caused the dayspring to know his place, That it might take hold of the ends of the earth, that the wicked might be shaken out of it" (JOB 38:12-13) KJV

This is the watch you command, every evil and wickedness to get out of your life and your destiny. This is the hour to speak to your challenges, storms and contrary winds to be averted. You completely eradicate wickedness and evil out of your day by declaring and commanding it to leave according to the scripture above. The scripture also says "Death and Life is in the power of the tongue" (Proverbs 18:21). It was during this watch that Jesus walked on water and commanded Peter to come by walking on the water, (Matthew 14:25-33). It is the hour of covering those in your sphere of influence under the canopy of his power.

5. FIFTH WATCH (6:00 AM TO 9:00 AM)

This watch is the first watch of the day, this is the time to ask God for his purpose and Will of the day. It is also the time for sanctification and consecration. It is the time to seek God for his divine direction, so he could order your steps in the path of righteousness and purity.

> "Consecrate yourself today to the Lord, that he may bestow a blessing on you this day" (Exodus 33:29)

> "Order my steps according to your word, and let not any iniquity have dominion over me" (Psalms 119:133)

At this watch you brake and deal with the power of sin, iniquity, and transgression over your life, you remove satanic veils and coverings of darkness, it is the hour of establishing divine counsel and purpose for your future, enacting covenants with the Lord to walk in his way and to keep his charge. It is the hour of walking in triumphant glory and dominion, establishing His kingdom for the advancement of divine and heavenly agenda.

> "Thus Saith the Lord of host, if thou wilt walk in my way, and if thou wilt keep my charge, then thou shalt also judge my house, and shalt also keep my courts and I will give you thee places to walk

among these that stand by" (Zachariah 3:7) KJV

6. SIXTH WATCH (9:00 AM to 12 noon)

It was during this hour that there was a massive outpouring upon the early church by the Holy Spirit (Acts 2:1-21). This hour is significant because it is the third hour of the day and the Jews used this hour to come together for corporate prayer and instruction at the temple, the third hour of the day is 9:00 AM, and nine is the number of birthing, and so at this hour whatever you are carrying in your spiritual womb, must be birthed, miracles, breakthrough, healings, favor, open doors, ministries, businesses, and ideas, must move from the abstract to become concrete. It also represents the nine gifts of the spirits, and so at this hour you pray that the Holy Spirit will release his power on you and within you and also to pray for his character to be formed in you, which is the fruits of the spirit remember is also nine. It is the hour of divine awakening and revival, personally and cooperatively in the body of Christ.

7. SEVENTH HOUR (12 Noon to 3:00 PM

This is the hour of redemption and deliverance from generational curses and ancestral yokes because prophetically and historically this was the hour when Christ was crucified on the cross and died reconciling man back to God and atoning and redeeming man from sin and curses, and given man absolute restoration of all things. This is the watch for restoration of what the enemy stole and took away from us.

This is the hour to deal with Satanic systems, governmental systems, economic systems, during this watch you pray for supernatural revelation and divine wisdom, rebuke every demonic and satanic spirits of darkness, over your city, life, destiny, ministry and your family, that the sun will rise and shine brightly over everything that concerns you.

"YOU will not be afraid of the terror by night, nor the arrow that flies by day, nor the pestilence that stalks in darkness, nor of the destruction (sudden death) that lays waste at noon" (Psalms 91:5-6).

8. EIGHTH WATCH (3:00 PM TO 6:00 PM)

This is the watch to deal with affliction, sickness, and disease, setting the captives free. Pray for the release of Signs and Wonders, miracles and healing over the earth that the bound will be loose and the oppress will go free, this is the watch you pray for God's compassion to be released on the earth and its inhabitants. You pray for the Glory of God to manifest.

It was this watch Peter and John entered the temple and at the gate healed the lame man in Jesus Name and the man stood and was praising God into the temple. (Acts 3:1-10)

Spiritual Warfare

"Put on the whole armour of God, that you may be able to stand against the wiles of the devil. For we wrestle not against flesh and blood, but against principalities, against powers, against the rulers of the darkness of this age, against spiritual wickedness in high places"
(Ephesians 6:11-12)

The Christian life is not simply believing in Jesus and living happily ever after. It would be nice if that were the case. However anyone who has sought to seriously follow the Lord has found it to be otherwise. Jesus said to his followers that life in this world would be marked by tribulation and opposition. That opposition comes to us in a large degree from the devil and a multitude of wicked spirits who form a united front against the kingdom of God.

Now I am certain that every Christian has experienced this apposition and some more accurately than others. I am also certain that many have not known that the source of the opposition was spiritual.

One of Satan most effective strategies is to keep us ignorant of the existence of this warfare, to disguise himself so well that we do not recognize what is actually taking place. As C.S. Lewis said in his preface to the screwtape letters: "The *demons hail with delight the materialist who disbelieves their existence.*" Although Lewis' statement might not apply to any of us directly because we are Christians, not materialists, it does apply in as much as, although we are Christians, quite often we live in oblivion to the spiritual realm that surrounds us.

Our purpose in this study is to be introduced to the reality of spiritual warfare, and in doing so to be helped on our way to victory in this battle.

THE OPPOSERS

We begin with a consideration of the inspiration behind the conflict, the devils and his angels. Who is the devil? Is he a real entity or just a mythological figure? The bible teaches that the devil is real person, a spirit being who was originally God's most glorious creature, but, by an act of rebellion, has become God's arch enemy (Isaiah 14). The Bible tells us that he is incredibly powerful, exceedingly intelligent, and immeasurably evil. Scripture also teaches that he is perpetually at war with God and His people.

He is the commander and chief of a multitude of creatures similar to himself. These creatures are referred to by Paul as *"principalities and powers, rulers of the darkness of this world, spiritual wickedness in high places."* All of these indicate organized opposition.

By way of analogy, consider the Roman Empire. Caesar sat in Rome and made policy based upon his counsel with the senate. The senators would pass the decision of the counsel down to the governors and rulers who will then implement their decisions. Likewise, within the kingdom of satan, there are those high ranking officials and those lower ranks that implement the policy.

The tenth chapter of Daniel's prophecy gives us insight into the kingdom of satan. (Daniel 10:1-14)

Notice what the angel said: *"the prince of the Persian kingdom resisted me twenty-one days."*

Cyrus was the king of Persia at that time, yet, he most certainly was not resisting the angelic messenger. The reference is to the spiritual power behind the Persian Empire. A similar thing is said in Isaiah 14 and Ezekiel 28 where prophets are prophesying against the kings of Babylon and Tyre. As they are prophesying, they suddenly and without explanation begin to address the spiritual powers behind the earthly rulers. Therefore we must also realize that the world we live in is not what it appears to be (essentially material), it also has a spiritual dimension and is actually governed by "wicked spirits in high places." It is imperative that we recognize the spiritual truth.

Let me cite one more example of this invisible kingdom from the New Testament. Do you remember when the Lord was being tempted? Satan showed Him all the kingdom of the world and their glory and said to him:

> *"All this authority I will give you, and their glory; for this has been delivered to me, and I give it to whomever I wish".*
>
> (Luke 4:6)

Jesus did not dispute satan's claim of authority over the kingdom of the world nor his ability t give them to whomever he wished. As a matter of fact, Jesus affirmed satan's claim when He later referred to him as "the ruler of this world" (John 14:30). These are biblical facts which we need to understand. I believe many Christians have been seduced into thinking the way that the secular person thinks, looking at everything as merely related to man and natural processes. However Paul says, "We wrestle not against flesh and blood". The conflict is ultimately with these spirit forces and unless we understand this we are defeated from the very unset.

The Battle

The next thing we need to consider is the intimate nature of the battle indicated by the term "wrestle". There are really two aspects of this spiritual warfare. There is the general aspect in which the collective forces of God are battling the collective forces of satan. Then there is also a very personal aspect where you and I are engaged in hand to hand combat with demonic spirits. It's a wrestling match. It's intimate. It's personal. It's deadly. As a Christian you are being studied, stalked and assaulted regularly.

Failure to realize this can result in your becoming a casualty in this battle. May be at this point you are saying "wait a minute; aren't you going a bit over board with this? What do you mean I'm being studied, stalked and assaulted by demons? This sounds fanatical."

I can assure you that I'm not being fanatical, but rather, scriptural. I'm simply stating what the Bible teaches generally and referring specifically to what is recorded in the case of Job.

Please see (Job 1:6-10)

You see, Satan had studied Job. He had stalked him. Very shortly he would assault him. Satan's tactics have not changed over the centuries. Today we are subject to the same kind of attacks Job experienced. I hope I'm not creating paranoia in anyone; that surely isn't my intention. My intention is to help you to see and understand the world and your personal experiences through a biblical lens. Christians today more than ever need a biblical world view, which includes a belief in and understanding of spiritual realms.

The Battle Is The Lord

Now that we've established the reality of spiritual warfare we need to know how we are to survive in this invisible battle. The first thing to remember is that "the battle is the Lord's", and therefore it is essential that we be *"strong in the Lord and in the power of his might"*.

(Ephesians 6:10)

We have no natural power with which to content with the forces of darkness. If I am to be victorious I must draw my strength from the Lord. It was my understanding that gave victory to men like David and Jehoshaphat. When David faced Goliath he made it clear that he stood in God's strength:

Please see: (I Samuel 17:45-47)

Likewise when Jehoshaphat cried to the Lord for deliverance from his enemies, the prophet, Jehaziel, responded: "Thus says the Lord to you: Do not be afraid nor dismayed because of this great multitude, for the battle is not yours, but God's" (2 Chronicles 20:15). It is critical that we remember this lest we be overcome with fear and discouragement.

The Weapon Of Our Warfare

Another important point to remember is that "the weapons of our warfare are not canal, but mighty in God."
(2 Corinthians 10:4-5)

What are the "weapons" God has given us? They are simply prayer, the word of God and worship. We must be thoroughly immersed in these if we are going to successfully fight the "good fight of faith." Later, we'll take an in-depth look at these "weapons that are mighty in God", but for now, we move on to a further consideration of the enemy.

READY OR NOT.....
YOU'RE IN THE BATTLE

There are so many that are simply not interested in hearing about spiritual warfare. Some feel that spiritual warfare is a special gift or calling, only for a small segment of Christians. I remember one lady asked me why is the enemy fighting me? Or a pastor who said he doesn't like battles and spiritual warfare.

Spiritual warfare however has nothing to with personality, gifting, calling or background. When we signed up to be Christians, we automatically entered into warfare. It's not a matter of preference. Spiritual warfare begins with recognizing that we are already in the midst of it.

Almost every Christian freely confesses that Jesus defeated the enemy at Calvary; however, the mental knowledge that Jesus defeated the devil and that we have authority over him is not enough. We continually allow satan, whom we know was defeated, to push us around and take advantage of us. We often act more like victims than the victors Christ intended us to be. As the children of God, we need never be victims. If we understand the biblical principles of spiritual warfare and how the enemy operates, and if we stand against him, we will overcome.

THE GOD OF THIS AGE

> *"Now there was a day when the sons of God came to present themselves before the Lord, and Satan[b] also came among them. And the Lord said to Satan, "From where do you come?" So Satan answered the Lord and said, "From going to and fro on the earth, and from walking back and forth on it"*
>
> (Job 1:6-7)

From this passage found in the book of Job, we see that our enemy, satan, is indeed alive and well on planet earth. Therefore the question is: what is he doing? The answer: a whole lot more than most people blame him for. Let's take a look at some of the devil's activity in the world.

The devil's activity is all over, you need to have discernment to see it all over the place, worldliness, ungodliness, homosexuality, disobedience, the lust of the flesh, the lust of the eye, hypocrisy, pride, fornication, infidelity, just to name a few.

But it doesn't stop there! Satan is also busy at work in the affairs of men. Whether it's international politics, the media, academia, the entertainment industry, or the fads and fashions of the world, his influence is felt. Paul referred to satan as "the prince of the power of the air, the spirit that now works in the children of disobedience" (Ephesians 2:2). From evolutionary theory to Marxist philosophy, from racial prejudice to multi-culturalism, from gang violence to world wars, from the sexual revolution to AIDS, from broken homes to the violent crime epidemic, from alcoholism to drug addiction, satan's work is evident. The hatred and violence, the death and destruction, the pain and misery, from the beginning of history until today are all to a large degree due to the activity of the devil. Truly as the Apostle John said "the whole world lies under the sway of the wicked one." (I John 5:14).

STRATEGIES OF THE DEVIL

> *"Put on the whole armor of God that you may be able to stand against the wiles of the devil for we do not wrestle against flesh and blood, but against principalities, against powers, against the rulers of the darkness of this age, against spiritual hosts of wickedness in the heavenly places. Above all, taking the shield of faith with which you will be able to quench all the fiery darts of the wicked one."*
> (Ephesians 6:11-12, 16)

The "wiles of the devil" and the "Fiery darts of the wicked one" although covering a broad range of activity are no doubt inclusive of satan's attack upon our mind and emotions. These attacks result in such experiences as condemnation, doubt, fear, evil thoughts and depression. Now I do not claim to understand how it is that satan and demons can access our minds and emotions, but that they can is clear both from scripture, and the testimony of many of God's servants throughout the long history of the church. Take for example what is recorded in 1 Chronicles 21:1, "Now satan stood up against Israel, and moved David to number Israel." When David was suddenly impressed to number the people, I doubt that he was aware that he was being influenced by satan, yet that is exactly what happened.

When we come to the New Testament, we find a similar instance with the apostle Peter recorded in Matthew 16:13-23. There Jesus asked the disciples "who do you say that I am?" Simon Peter answered and said, "You are the Christ, the son of the living God."

Then as Jesus proceeded to tell them about His coming rejection by the leaders at Jerusalem, and His subsequent execution, peter, well-meaning but misguided, took Jesus aside and began to rebuke him saying, "Far be it from you, Lord, this shall not happen to you!"

The response of Jesus to Peter illustrates my point. Jesus turned and said to Peter, "Get behind me, satan! You are on offense to me, for you are not mindful of the things of God, but the things of men."

Peter was mentally under the influence of Satan; his thought at this point was satanically inspired.

Peter's response and the subsequent rebuke of Christ is all the more remarkable in that we are told that his earlier confession was a matter of divine revelation.

Perhaps the most tragic example of satan's attack upon the mind and emotions is found in John 13:2 where we read; "the devil put it into the heart of Judas Iscariot to betray Jesus."

In each of these cases, we see the enemy's ability to influence the way we think and feel. Having established that fact, we now want to take a closer look at some of the "wiles of the devil" in order to become aware of and avoid being ensnared by them.

Condemnation Of The Devil

A common tactic of the devil is to make you feel cut off from God's love and forgiveness. This occurs most often after some failure on your part. It is then that condemnation usually strikes. However, it is important to distinguish between conviction and condemnation, on the other hand, produces guilt and leaves the victim with a sense of hopelessness.

The devil moves in and begins to suggest to you that God is fished with you; he will say' "you've gone too far this time". He implies that forgiveness is unavailable to you. You might even have overwhelming feelings that God has abandoned you and that He no longer loves you. All of this is typical of the "fiery dots of the enemy can only be overcome by taking up the shield of faith, faith in the word of God. The power of condemnation ties in satan's ability to deceive us into thinking that God is the one condemning us. For after all, if God is against us, who can be for us? However, this is the exact opposite of what is true! In Romans 8:1 Paul says: "There is therefore no condemnation to those who are in Christ Jesus..." and then in verse 31 he says: "...God is for us, who can be against us?" In verses 33-34 he asks, "Who shall bring a change against God's elect? It is God who justifies. Who is he who condemns? It is Christ who died, and furthermore is also risen, who is even at the right hand of God, who also make intercession for us." The accusing thoughts, those condemning feelings come from "the accuser of the brethren." It is only by confidence in the blood of the lamb that we can overcome satanic condemnation.

If you've sinned, don't let the devil drive you away from the Lord through condemnation. Instead, confess your sin and remember that "He is faithful and just to forgive your sins and to cleanse you from all from all unrighteousness" (I John 1:9).

Painting Doubt

Another of the devils darts is plant doubts in our minds. Satan will try to get you to doubt everything from God's existence to your salvation. He is especially concerned with casting doubt on the word of God. An important thing to remember on this subject is that there is a difference between the temptation to doubt God and the sin of unbelief. It's possible to be plagued by doubt and yet innocent of the sin of unbelief.

The great English preacher Charles Spurgeon was very familiar with this particular form of temptation. He said "My peculiar temptation has been constant unbelief. I know that God's promise is true. Yet does this temptation incessantly assail me, doubt Him, distrust Him, etc." Spurgeon of course, resisted the temptation, but his statement indicated that he struggled constantly in this area.

Recognize it as one of the devil's tactics and stand firm on the word of God.

It's alright to ask questions. It's through asking questions that we learn. Through honest questions you can turn your temptations to doubt into opportunities to grow in your understanding of the Lord, His Word and His way. At the end of every honest question you will find that God is true even as Paul concludes in Romans 3:4, "Let God be true and every man a liar."

FEAR

Fear, it is the apprehension, anxiety of the unknown, when you are anxious of an unknown danger. Fear is also the state of extreme apprehension, usually when courage has fled.

Fear is another 'wiles of the devil', and he uses it as one of his tactics. He threatens evil consequences upon those who would trust and obey the Lord. When the 18th century revivalist George Whitefield called upon his friend John Wesley to take over his open-air preaching ministry, John was suddenly struck with the impression that if he were to do so, he would die. Having sought divine guidance by randomly opening his Bible on four different occasions, the scriptures seemed to confirm his fear of death. His fears proved to be nothing more than the work of the devil seeking to prevent him from entering into the work that God has called in to. It was actually through the acceptance of that invitation that John Wesley entered his evangelistic career which lasted more than fifty years and resulted in the conversion of tens of thousands and the forming of the Methodist church.

A second example of this fear tactic is seen in the story of Rabbi who through various circumstances came to believe that Jesus is the Messiah of Israel. When he received Christ he realized that he needs to choose a day on which to make a public confession of his faith by being baptized. His story of the events that transpired on the day of his baptism amply illustrates the devil's attempt to hinder God's work in us through this fear tactic. The devil uses fear to frighten you and paralyze you of your courage and power. Satan will threaten you just as Soul threatened. But that is all he is able to so because *"Greater is He who is in you, than he who is in the world"* (I John 4:4). Again, *"If God be for us who can be against us?"* (Romans 8:31). Don't let the enemy keep you out of the will of God through this fear tactic. Remember, *"God has not given us a spirit of fear, but of power love, and a sound mind"* (2 Timothy 1:17). Our heavenly father has our eternal best in mind so yield to Him without fear. Watch what he will do. The Lord knows best.

Satan Thoughts and Imaginations

Another manifestation of the "wiles of the devil" is evil thoughts. Have you even been in prayer and had your mind suddenly assaulted by blasphemous thoughts? Have you ever been worshipping and had pornographic images flash across your mind? Have you ever gone through a period of time in which your mind was obsessed by deplorable thoughts, thoughts that sickened and oppressed you, thoughts that you longed to be delivered from, thoughts of sexual immortality, murder or suicide? If so you are not alone.

An experience from the life of Charles Spurgeon serves as an illustration. Having gone through a prolonged period of blasphemous assault upon his mind and being near the point of despair, he was now questioning even his salvation (for after all, how could a true Christian think such thoughts?). He finally confided in his grandfather who also happened to be a minster of the gospel. His grandfather asked him one simple question: "do you take pleasure in those thoughts?" Young Spurgeon replied: "No, I hate them!" his grandfather responded, "then have nothing to do with them. Do not won them because they are not yours, but the devil's."

As nature abhors a vacuum, so our mind cannot long remain empty. God thoughts leave no room for bad thoughts.

Depression

Depression is perhaps the most devastating of the "wiles of the devil" in as much as the devil gathers up all of the things we've discussed (condemnation, doubt, fear, evil thoughts and imaginations), wraps them in despair and leaves you with an overwhelming sense of hopelessness.

We also have many examples from church history of those who suffered from depression, William Cowper, the great English poet and hymn writer, battled his entire life with manic depression.

Charles Spurgeon said: "I, of all men, am perhaps the subject of the deepest depression at times.... Depression so fearful I hope none of you ever get to such extremes of wretchedness as I go to."

So we see that God's people are not exempt from depression. Everyone suffers from depression from time to time, some more frequently and more severely than others. The question is then: How do we deal with depression?

First of all, we need to know what's causing it. There are basically four types of depression. There is depression that is organic in nature (a bodily malfunction, i.e. hormonal or chemical imbalances). Then there is a circumstantial depression, the problems of life have gotten you down. Some depression is directly related to sin. And finally there is depression that is direct result of satanic activity.

We move now to consider our final aspect of the devil's war against us. Laziness, we have time to do everything else but prayer, it is the tactics of the enemy to defeat us; that is why you don't only pray when you feel like it, but you also pray when you don't feel like it. There is absolutely nothing in the world that can substitute prayer, prayer is everything and everything is prayer, don't let the devil keep you down, rise and war, rise and fight! We have won the battle, praise God!

BE CAREFUL OF WHO STANDS AT YOUR GATE

The person that stands at the gate, has the power and authority to decide what comes in and what comes out, he has the power to disallow and allow, he also the ability to shut in and shot out.

Whoever stands at your gate will determine, what comes in your life and what exist out of it. When an evil man stands at your gate, he will stop good things from coming into your life and he will allow evil and wickedness to come in, that is why you can't be oblivious of who is standing at your gate.

The plan of the enemy is to takeover your gate and when he takes over your gate, he has taken over your life, my questions to you is who is standing at your Family gate, because the person that stands at the Family gate determines who goes up and who comes down, who succeed, and who doesn't who is standing at your career gate? Who is standing at your financial gate?? "Saul got wind of their plot,

Day and Night they watched the gate to kill him' **(Acts 9:24) NKJV.**

When they wanted to kill Saul who later became Paul, guess where they were looking for him to kill him at the gate, the scripture says they watched day and night to see him come out or come in through the gate so they could kill him, when the enemy wants to eliminate you, he targets your gate, don't allow the enemy to stop you or finish you at your gate, take a stand and push back the works of the enemy.

"For he has strengthened the bars of your gate, he has blessed your sons within you. **(Psalm 147:13) NKJV.** The Lord himself energizes and strengthens our gates so there cannot be an intruder, invader, wickedness coming into our dwelling, when the gate is strengthen there cannot be opposition, and resistance cannot prevail". "Your choice valleys were filled with chariots, and horseman set themselves in array against the gate" **(Isaiah 22:7) NKJV.** Let the Angels take a fix position at your gate and let Chariots of fire guard your gate.

Satanic Gates

While there are physically gates, they are also spiritual gates, there are heavenly gates, and there are satanic gates.

"So the sword whirl in their cities, destroys the bars of their gates, and devour them in their fortress" **(Hosea 11:6) NKJV.**

Within the city there is satanic counsels against you and your family, causing havoc and pain, and God is saying enough! Is enough! but my Sword will destroy all these cities that are conspiring against you, working against your progress, and I will demolish their satanic gates and consume them because of their evil counsels.

May every satanic gate working against your advancement catch fire and be bent into ashes in Jesus Name, and may the people there in be scattered by thunder and lighting.

"And I tell you that you are Peter (which mean "rock"), and upon this rock I will build my church and the gates of hell will not overcome it) **Matthew 16:18 (NIV).**

To stop the gates of hell one must fight, one must contend, one must take a stand through prayer and spiritual warfare, that is the only language the devil and hades understand.

"It came about when it was time to shut the gates at dark that the men went out, I do not know where the men went. Pursue them quickly, for you will overtake them" **(Joshua 2:5) NKJV**

Joshua said go after those who were supposed to be shutting the gate but have left it open for the enemy to come in, capture them and destroy and kill them. The enemy operates in the dark and at night, they decided to keep the gate open at night, the time of operations, so they can come in easily.

Any conspiracy at your gate to allow the enemy to come in and destroy, steak and kill. May their hands not perform their enterprise and may they be destroyed in their craftiness, your gateman will not align with your enemy in Jesus Name!

Today I stand at my watch and I command Satanic and demonic gates to be shattered by the hammer of the word. "For he has shattered gates of bronze and has broken iron bars" (Psalm 107:16) NKJV

"The mighty man of Babylon have ceased fighting, they stay in the strongholds, their strength is exhausted, they are becoming like women, their dwelling places are set on fire, the bars of gates are broken "Jeremiah 51:30" NKJV

Entering Into New Gates

"Open to me the gates of righteousness, I shall enter through them, I shall give thanks to the Lord" (Psalm 118:19)

Every gate designed to bring you joy, happiness, prosperity, and favor may the Lord open it for you and may you enter with ease. If there is a gate of righteousness, then there is a gate of elevation, these season of your life, may you come into that gate, when the Lord opens the gate he watches until you have entered into it, every gate you have missed entering, I release you right now to enter into it.

Spiritual battles are not won by physical gadget, it is not also won in the natural through political processes, it is won in the spirit before it is manifested in the flesh. Before you can displace satanic rulers in the natural world, you need to first displace satanic rulers in the spirit realm. We must first cast down vain imagination in the spirit before we can change the paganism world view in the natural.

Understand The Spiritual Realm

The spiritual realm is another world, which consist of God, angelic beings, Satan and his agents. The spiritual realms is the very real realm in which, God, angelic beings, Satan and demonic beings exist. The scripture teaches us that there are two realms of existence, these are the natural and the spiritual realms. "While we look not at these things which are seen but at the things which are not seen, for the things which are seen are temporal, but the things which are not seen are eternal" **(2 Corinthians 4:18) NKJV.**

The natural realm is the one in which we live, work, and play, but God created men to be eternal citizens of the spiritual realm. It is on this spiritual realm that the forces of light and darkness do battle, Worship God or Satan and dominate our minds. It is amazing that there is the acceptance of the reality of the spirit world among Christians almost all over the world. I have heard of many instances of people interacting with the spirits in Europe, Asia, Africa, American and Australia, but the most disturbing is the fact that though there is no awareness of reality of the spirit world, there are many believers who don't adequately understand the biblical perspective of the spirit world, because we don't have a proper understanding of what the Bible teaches believers frequently engage themselves in occultie activity without realizing that what they are doing is wrong.

"If there rise amongst you a prophet or a dreamer of dreams and giveth a sign or a wonder and the sign or the wonder comes to pass whereof he spoke unto the saying, let us go after other God's which thou hast not know, and let us serve them; thou shalt not hearken unto the words of that prophet or the dreamer of dreams; for the Lord your God tested you, to know whether ye love the Lord your God with all of your heart and with all of your soul" (Deuteronomy 13:3) **NKJV**

From the above scripture, we can therefore conclude that regarding the spiritual practitioners, the judgement criteria is not whether their deeds come to pass, not whether or not it is good, but where does their power come from??

Also, in the spirit world, there is two powerful but unequal beings: There is God and Satan. God through the Holy Spirit is calling man to external life through Jesus Christ. Satan through he's lies, half-truths, deception, embodied in his demonic being is working to prevent man from having external life with God. Satan isn't going to cure your fever, heal your child, make you pregnant, and find your lost property for you, all for free. He will definitely demand something in exchange for his help, however most people who consult these practitioners never know that they are exchanging one problem for another bigger problem.

These are the other books by the same author:

- Another Level of Prayer
- Principles of Purpose and Adversity
- Still Standing
- Undercover Generation
- Breaking satanic cycles
- Enemy at the Gate

To contact the author, please call this number 770-944-1934 or visit:

www.raphaelgrantministry.com
www.eagleschapel.com

Printed in the USA
CPSIA information can be obtained
at www.ICGtesting.com
JSHW020215101123
51593JS00005B/42